How to Attune Yourself to

Reiki

the Cosmology Way

How to Attune Yourself to

Reiki

the Cosmology Way

The Science of Universal Energy

John Campbell

ISBN 1-84409-028-0

British Library Cataloguing-in-Publication Data.

A catalogue record for this book is available from the British Library.

Cover and interior design by Thierry Bogliolo

Reiki symbols by Tomoko Kamimura

Printed by WS Bookwell, Finland

Published by

Findhorn Press

305a The Park, Findhorn

Forres IV36 3TE, Scotland

Tel 01309 690582

Fax 01309 690036

e-mail: info@findhornpress.com

www.findhornpress.com

Contents

Preface

This book is set out in an easy to use format, designed to give the reader insight into how Reiki can be used in daily life. Reiki gives us the ability to heal ourselves and others on a physical, emotional, and spiritual level. It does this through the use of symbols to empower the sacred self with the healing energy available to all.

You will learn how to attune yourself to Reiki, which is traditionally thought of as impossible. These easy step-by-step exercises are formulated to open the door to higher consciousness, making Reiki available to anyone. Healing is a universally available gift and it is my wish that everyone knows how best to use it.

These pages cover the three levels of Reiki and also explore the world of spirituality. The intention is for you, the reader, to develop self-empowerment. Reiki can help you on your own personal life journey, as well as benefiting those around you.

Disclaimer

Healing and Medicine are two very different disciplines and the law requires the following disclaimer. The information in this book is not medicine but healing and does not constitute medical advice. In case of serious illness consult the practitioner of your choice.

Introduction

I was born in the North East of England on the tenth of July 1962 to Mary and Joseph Campbell. I am the youngest son of four siblings. South Shields was a relatively small industrial town in the sixties and seventies and boasted a coal mine and several small shipyards. The school I went to was typical of the time, built in the late fifties with classrooms that couldn't handle the number of children born during the baby boom years. The school was rough and bullying was rife. I was sexually abused on a number of occasions by a fifth former who lived at the top of my street during my first year of high school. I can remember thinking of the shame I would feel if anyone found out that this was happening to me. He was finally caught sexually assaulting another lad in the street and his family moved soon after. I left school in 1978 and swore to myself that no one would ever bully or abuse me again.

At 19 I bought my first motorcycle and was soon enjoying the freedom having my own set of wheels gave me. A few years later my self-confidence built up enough to hitch hike throughout Europe and Australia by myself.

On the 18th August 1988 I crushed my left foot in a motorcycle accident and was told that I would not walk without the aid of a walking stick for the rest of my life. Since conventional medicine had nothing to offer me I turned instead to complimentary therapies. I used Acupuncture and Kinesiology as well as Reiki healing and threw away the walking stick. I also learned the basics of these techniques and developed my own healing techniques along the way. I am writing with direct experience of how these healing techniques have worked for me, as well as benefited many of my clients.

In 1997 I went through the process of a very difficult separation. Some times life throws you a curve ball and you find that the best thing to do is get out of the way. I found myself driving aimlessly throughout Australia searching for something that I knew was there – but didn't know what it was. I managed to drive from Adelaide to Brisbane in two days and found myself camping on top of the Binna Burra Mountains for two nights. Eventually the ticks and leaches led me back to civilization real quick.

Coming from the north east of England and it being Friday night, I was on a mission to go out and have a few drinks to suppress my frustration at the situation I was in. That night I was introduced to a lady who was running self-development courses and I figured that since I was in a bit of a predicament as far as my life and marriage were concerned, I had nothing to lose by going along.

Talking to Crystals!

The course was called 'Introduction to Channel' and I hadn't a clue what I had gotten myself into. I have to remind you that I am from an industrial background and this course was on another planet as far as I was concerned. I thought of asking for my money back, but I was in Brisbane and no-one back home would know what I was doing – so decided to carry on with the workshop with an open mind.

The first section of the course was guided meditation, which I found to be quite relaxing. The next section was crystal readings. I looked in horror at the course coordinator and thought that she deserved to be locked up in the funny farm. She placed an amethyst crystal in my hand and asked me to close my eyes and talk to the crystal.

What followed was such a shock. The crystal felt as if it was going to burn a hole into the palm of my hand, my whole arm ached with pain, and then out of the blue an inner voice – as loud as can be – said "Let go of the past". The coordinator asked me to meditate on what healing qualities an amethyst crystal has and my inner voice piped up again, saying: "Amethyst can ease emotional pain and bring clarity into ones life".

I did the same exercise with three different crystals with the same clear results. I couldn't believe that I was 'reading' crystals, and wanted to find out more about what I was doing and how.

One side of me thought that I was absolutely bonkers and the other side felt excited at this newfound gift. The next day I raced into the workshop and couldn't wait to see what else I could achieve. I was introduced to my spirit Guides through guided meditation. The experience was amazing! I was told that I was going to be a healer and a teacher. I also discovered how to listen to my highest guides of universal love and light, who have also been described as the Ascended Masters. Unfortunately I was unable to save my marriage, but I was able to save my life.

This course started me on a journey of self-discovery. I began to live an alternative life style, on a quest to find the reality of seemingly obscure healing techniques. I feel very blessed that I have had the opportunity to live in total isolation on the top of mountains (yes, I went back again) and in caves throughout the country of Australia. This gave me the ability to enhance my skills as a teacher and healer and to seek and grown within; listening to inner teachers and communicating with guides. I have lived and breathed these techniques for the last four years and they have certainly changed my life for the better.

Please understand that everything I am writing about is real and reveals the power that we all have within us. You haven't lived my life, but this book will open you up to the power that is within you, without having to go through the process of living an isolated lifestyle. To channel the energy of the universe is to go on a journey within oneself. The inner self is where your power is waiting to manifest into the reality of life.

What is Reiki – and what is it not?

I have worked with a few Reiki teachers and masters and have explored this way of healing for many years. Being a working class boy I like to know how things work and to understand what is happening – and to be able to pass that information onto others in an easily understandable way. That is my aim with this book. In my exploration of Reiki I found some confusion and had to find my way through it.

In my opinion, some Reiki masters look upon Reiki as a little understood spiritual form of healing – leaving the basics to a wild and mystical ideology, with little or no comprehension of what or how it works.

There are people who think that once they attain Reiki three they become some sort of master of the Universe and then allow their huge egos to take over – diminishing their level of awareness of their spiritual self or life. Some teachers like the power status that they seem to attain with Reiki and they become controlling masters. Others will teach students the basics but never allow them access to their full knowledge – keeping some level of higher mystical status and avoiding difficult questions at all costs. Through my experience, if the teacher avoids the question they don't know the answer!

Of course there are also some very spiritual and accomplished Reiki Masters out there, who have really 'done their work' and wish to share all they have with others.

Who ever we choose to teach us, there lies our lesson. In other words, if we choose a teacher that is controlling, we will find that we are controlled. And likewise if we choose an empowered and open teacher, we will attract those same qualities.

The question has to be asked: Why pay large sums of money for Reiki, when you can experience Reiki for very little money exchange? The prices for and duration of courses to attain the same certificates vary dramatically. Do some people think that the more they pay the better they will be?

Through teaching Reiki for many years, I have encountered numerous different symbols that may confuse the average teacher – and pupil. The symbols in this book cover the more unified symbols that I have encountered, and are from the book written by Diane Stein (one of the more informative books available on the subject of Reiki).

As a Reiki teacher, I have come across three different histories of Reiki, and each one is very different to the other, and – in my opinion – quite irrelevant. Many Reiki masters seem to get caught up in a heritage format, as if it will make them a better healer if someone teaches them with an accredited bloodline, or is a far removed distant cousin to Takata (the lady who brought Reiki to the western world). Some Reiki masters seem to value their knowledge by the amount of money they have spent on acquiring their Reiki healing technique.

There are currently two teaching formats with Reiki healing, called Usui Shiki Ryoho and Seishem. Each teaching format is slightly different to the other. In my estimation, if Reiki Masters quibble about which one is the greater, they are avoiding the question: Why do these techniques work? I have endeavoured all of my spiritually aware life to access the knowledge of how these techniques work on the human body.

With this book, I will endeavour to show you how easy it is to heal with your hands. It is irrelevant if you have learned Reiki over ten years or two weeks, we all have the ability to use these skills.

Cosmology Method

Through years of study and experience I have developed my own 'hands on healing technique' called the Cosmology Healing Method and have many testimonials stating the positive effects these techniques have – particularly on skeletal and spinal problems. Keeping spirituality a reality is my gift and I intend to live my life with two feet firmly grounded upon this earth. I believe we are all healers and encourage you to trust in your own abilities.

As humans we are here to develop throughout our lives on a continual basis on all levels: spiritually, mentally and physically. Change comes through lessons we all have to learn. We are all unique, with our own qualities and special gifts that only we can access as our divine right and birthright. Each person that lives and breathes has the ability to access the inner strength of love and self-empowerment that can be attained through the use of Reiki.

We all wish to love and heal others instinctively. If someone hurts himself or herself our instinctive wish is to help, we are all healers by instinct and our positive nature is with us all. It is only fear that prevents us from helping others in a positive way. We all wish to help and be helped on deeper levels.

I have written this book about Reiki to develop an understanding as I see it. These techniques have a proven formula that works to gain greater knowledge of the sacred self. We are all different and we will gain different levels of awareness through the use of this book. Everyone who reads these pages may come to very different conclusions about what Reiki really is to them. What I hope you gain from this book is an understanding of how these techniques can benefit you in your own way.

Traditionally people would have to source a Reiki teacher to be attuned to Reiki and I do not discourage doing this. However, I wish to draw awareness to the self-attuning process and make Reiki widely available to all.

The standard way of attuning to Reiki is through another Reiki Master, who has already been attuned to the symbols of Reiki. This can sometimes cause what is called a clearing – a process of clearing negative energy that has been passed through the attuning process.

We all have lessons – even Reiki Masters – and as we are attuned to the symbols of Reiki we can collect negative energy from the person attuning us. Through each attuning process there is a slight element of the self that can flow from one person to the other, unless the Reiki Master has learned to completely cleanse his or her own energy first.

The self-attuning process will give you the ability to attune to your lesson and help clear negativity. By attuning you to your lesson it can help you to break negative cycles as well as help you to rise above negative karmic issues. Through this step-by-step process you are effectively attuning to the strength that is within you, without having to be affected by other people's lessons in the attuning process.

I strongly recommend that you read the pages of this book once through before attempting the exercises. The reason for this is to give you a good understanding that there is nothing to fear and to release any expectations before doing the exercises.

There is only positive growth to be gained from reading this book. Reiki works from the universal life force energy, which is the energy of unconditional love and acceptance.

Reiki Reversed

Traditionally, Reiki is taught in levels of growth that will develop a pupil in stages: Reiki level one, then two, and three. The understanding being that to undertake level three before level one will be too much for anyone to handle and bring on a clearing. I believe this can be so if you are attuned the traditional way, but not when you self-attune.

Reiki is a healing formula and cannot be used to hurt another person or you. The worst that could happen is Reiki would do nothing. By reading the book through before doing the exercises, you will gain understanding of what Reiki is as taught through the levels of Reiki level one and two.

However, to endeavour to learn Reiki we have to learn how to attune ourselves to Reiki first. This means to effectively understand this book we have to first go through the attuning process which is Reiki level three, which will connect us to our spiritual line – or Reiki energy. Level two will connect us to our emotions and emotional healing. And Reiki level one will connect us to our physical self.

This book is written to help you learn the attuning process first, in order to align the healing energy through you with the use of the symbols. The symbols have been structured to balance the energy throughout the chakra system, so all seven symbols can be utilised for the best effect to promote healing.

Once you are self attuned to Reiki you can then endeavour to move forward and perform the rest of the exercises through Reiki levels one and two. Going through the attuning process will help to align the healing energy through your chakra points, so you can feel the subtle changes in your body and your hands. Performing the attuning process first will give you the ability to feel the Reiki energy on your own level.

The more you can release your expectations of what will happen through a healing session, the more relaxed you and the person receiving healing will feel.

You may feel the Reiki energy as a cold sweat or a slight tingle flowing through the fingers. Whatever you feel will be on your own level and may be different to what others feel. Remember, we are all healers by instinct and we are all unique.

If you have been attracted to this book I believe that you will find a message within its covers. As you go through the steps of the self-attuning process, you will discover a message hidden within the symbols. This may come in the form of a feeling, a voice talking to you from within, or visualization. Please acknowledge what you are thinking and feeling as you attune yourself to the symbols.

Each symbol has been blessed to open the door to the healing consciousness. If you have already gone through the attuning process and learned the symbols of Reiki, you may find they are slightly different to the symbols I show in this book. Please understand that the energy behind the symbols will be the same. If you look at the word 'happiness' for example, the same word has different pronunciations and spellings in different languages but has the same energy behind it.

We all have the ability to heal ourselves. When we hurt ourselves we cover our pain with our hands. When our children are in pain we cover their pain with our hands, or kiss it better, in other words 'give it love.' Universal energy is unconditional love and acceptance. This is a natural instinct, which we have inherited from our distant past. The process of 'hands on healing' is nothing new, just something many have forgotten.

The purpose of this book is to align the self-healing energy that we all possess with the Reiki symbols, and to attune these symbols to our inner vibration. I have been blessed with this knowledge as a Universal Channel, with direct communication to my devoted Spirit Guides as my teachers.

Reiki courses today can vary from teacher to teacher, with different disciplines or heritages. In my opinion Reiki is healing and it really doesn't matter what discipline you follow as long as your *intention* to heal yourself, or others, with Reiki is genuine.

In my estimation Reiki is an excellent healing technique and should be available to all people who are open minded enough to accept alternative therapies into their lives. With this book I will endeavour to show you how easy it is to heal with your hands.

Reiki works on the Electromagnetic Vibration of the human body. Humans are huge energy systems and once you access the understanding that we are energy, and anything we do or think is energy based, it will be easy to understand how Reiki works on the physical, emotional and spiritual body.

The human body is very similar to a nine volt battery. The human body works off direct current and follows the same principals of any electrical circuit: positive to negative, or earth. I will show you how this works by telling stories through this book and keeping things very simple and easy to understand.

Chapter 1

About Reiki

The formula that makes the Reiki Healing method so very effective is that it empowers *four main levels of energy* during the attuning process (a unique process performed with the seven Reiki symbols). The four levels are:

Goddess Healing

The symbols empower the recipient to the energy of the Earth and the realm of the Goddess through their hands and feet

Divine Healing

The symbols empower the yellow (solar plexus) chakra, which is the energy of the Divine Self. This raises the recipient's vibration, releasing fear and enhancing love of the self.

Emotional Healing

The symbols empower self-healing related to our thoughts and feelings through our indigo (third eye) chakra, which is the realm of the inner healer or Reiki Guide. This will help balance emotions, release fear and enhance perceptions.

Universal Connection (God)

The symbols empower the universal life force energy that is located through our crown chakra. Universal energy is unconditional love and acceptance.

The Nine Principles

The nine principles of Reiki are what I consider to be 'laws' that govern the attuning process. By understanding and living your life with these guiding principles you will be acting for the highest good of yourself and all others.

1. Intention

We are all supreme and divine and spiritually we are all equal. We have the freedom of choice and free will to live this life as we choose. We have the divine right to create our own Universe with the use of our thoughts and feelings. When we state our intention to heal another person, we align ourselves with the energy of the Universe and the energy of the Highest Guides of the light. We come from love and when we die we go to love. As we experience life we source love. The purpose of the Highest Guides of the light is to take us to love through life.

The principal Law of intention is to intend and align the energy of Reiki to pass on to us in the form of unconditional love and acceptance, thus releasing any fear that is within us. Fear comes in the form of thoughts and once our fear is released we become enlightened – or *lightened* of our fears.

II. Enlightenment

To align with the energy of enlightenment one needs to state an intention to be healed. This aligns us with energy on a Universal magnitude, which is infinite, unconditional love and wisdom. We all have access to this love and wisdom – believe it or not you have a Universal consciousness as a divine right and birthright.

As humans we all think a lot – just listen to the continual stream of thought in your mind. And when we are stressed or worried about situations we think about them on an almost continual basis. We are enlightened when we have the answer to the situation that is worrying and stressing us. And the answers are there for us if we can open ourselves to them.

Would you say that Buddha was enlightened? And would you say that Christ was enlightened? Yes, of course you would. However, Christ was ridiculed, tortured, whipped, stoned and crucified for his beliefs. And have you heard the old Buddhist saying: "Before enlightenment pick up sticks and fetch water, after enlightenment pick up sticks and fetch water." Enlightenment comes from within and does not necessitate a specific saintly role in life or even an easy passage along life's journey. With enlightenment our perceptions change – not necessarily our external world.

Some people think that their life will become easier if they are enlightened, like being hit by a magic wand. To be enlightened doesn't necessarily mean that your lessons in life will get easier; it does mean that you will follow the light of love that is your true potential and destiny in this lifetime. Enlightenment comes from within to give a better understanding of who and what we are.

III. Transference

What you say and think creates energy. We think in the region of 45,000 to 75,000 thoughts per day. These thoughts create energy. When we think to our past and all that has occurred over our lives we are drawing on the energy of that time. Positive and negative thoughts create positive and negative actions. Acknowledge your thoughts from the past and acknowledge what is happening to you in the now. We are all divine and we are responsible for all the things that happen to us in our life.

IV. Karma

How we react to the environment creates a karmic effect upon us. Transference is about what we transfer out into our environment in the way of actions and thoughts and what is transferred back to us. Positive actions create positive karma and negative actions create negative karma.

All things have purpose and meaning, from the smallest of insects to the largest of coincidences. We create our own experiences with our desires, thoughts and actions. We are what we think we are, directly associated with our perception of how we relate to our environment. If, for example, we wish to control our environment we will have an experience of the environment controlling us, until we have learned the lesson and become harmonious with our environment.

V. Balance

As human beings we are emotional creatures and our own self-esteem creates our relationship to our environment, which in turn dictates to us our health and well being. Balance is to be at one with our own world and at one with all that is. If we act negatively towards our environment we will create a negative environment – this is what is generally known as cause and effect. Understanding this principle law can create a harmonious lifestyle for all.

VI. Cause and Effect

Wherever there is an action there is a reaction. Look at what you are thinking and what is happening around you in your life. You will find it's directly related to how you feel about yourself. What goes around comes around. If you feel anger toward someone or something in your environment you will find anger directed towards you (when the truth is you are only angry at yourself).

Cause and Effect can be used to explain how we create our own Universe with our mind. When we are in love, it is as if the whole world is in love with us. When we are angry it is as if the whole world is out to get us. When we love someone we transfer positive thoughts between each other. This positive energy then flows out to our environment. When we are in love we feel as if all our problems are small because someone is prepared to show us love and acceptance. When we are angry at someone it's because we did not receive love and acceptance.

VII. Acceptance

The principle Law of Acceptance is to accept yourself as you are. To source acceptance from your environment and those in it will show you your imperfections, by first hand experience. The environment is a reflection of our thoughts and feelings. If we desire to be accepted by the environment we will find that we are not getting acceptance in a way that we desire. We may find that the more we try to get accepted the more we are pushed away. Acceptance has to come from within and flow out to the environment. Understand that your environment will not be perfect, the people in it will never be perfect, and you will never be perfect. To accept yourself as you are is to say, "I am what I am". Once you have accepted yourself you will have the ability to start moving with the universal flow.

VIII. Universal Flow

To observe universal flow is to observe life from a universal perspective of unconditional love and acceptance. We all have the freedom of choice and free will to live life as we choose. To go with the universal flow is to choose love and acceptance of the self; to love and accept yourself as you are, unconditionally. No matter what you have done throughout your life, the universe loves you unconditionally. No matter how you look or feel about yourself, the universe loves you unconditionally. The keys to the universe are not obtained through pain or a desire for acceptance by others. The keys to the universe come from loving yourself as you are now. You are here living this life because the universe loves you for you.

The universe is expanding and we must expand with it. The universe, cosmos, planets and the earth create energy and life reacts to it. You the planets and the universe are one; all things in it are connected as one living entity. This is the energy of life force. Accept the love that you are and be a greater force in life.

IX. Life Force

Reiki is Universal Life Force Energy. Life force is energy given off by life itself. The trees, animals and all living things – including the Solar system – emanate life force. We are all connected to all things. To appreciate our planet and all things in it is to appreciate ourselves in perfect harmony with all things, and to be totally harmonious and balanced within.

How Reiki Works

Reiki healing is a form of vibrational healing. Vibrational healing works on the electro-magnetic energy flow of the human body. The human body is similar to a nine volt battery, it works off direct current and comes under the same principals and laws of any electrical circuit: electricity flows from positive to earth. Vibrational healing techniques work on the electrical circuit of the human body.

If we where to purchase a brand new car, we would expect to drive up a steep hill without any problems. But if the car was twenty years old we may get a bit of a reduction in speed and a few noises and groans emanating from the ageing body of the car. There is a similarity with the ageing of human bodies. As we age, our electrical circuit ages with us. As we go through life, we find our own personal hills more difficult to overcome.

You could compare the chakra system to a car battery. A car battery has separate cells containing distilled water and acid to allow the electrical current to flow from one cell to another. This is very similar to the primary chakra system. The primary chakra system flows positive energy through our seven primary chakra cells, from the crown chakra to the base – or root – chakra, down to earth.

Positive energy then flows through the secondary chakra system, via our meridian lines. Meridian lines are what are used in the ancient Chinese art of acupuncture. They are our equivalent to electrical cables – connecting the energy flow to all parts of the body.

Thoughts and Emotions

The electrical system of the human body is directly connected to our thoughts. When we feel happy we flow with positive energy and our auric colours are bright and vibrant. If we worry, we get run down, and if we worry for long periods of time we will find our health deteriorating.

Imagine what would happen if we were to leave the car lights on overnight, we would most probably find the car battery flat in the morning, with little or no positive electrical current held within the cells of the battery. Looking at the battery cells you may discover that the fluid has drained quite considerably so that one or all of the cells have emptied, causing the battery to be virtually useless until recharged. Similarly, when we worry or are under stress – when we don't switch off – we drain our chakra system, and each level has its own separate purpose in relation to our well being.

Chapter 2

The Chakras

The electrical vibration of the human body is governed by our chakra system that works off three levels: the primary chakra system, the secondary meridian chakra system, and the third, auric level (which is projected out from our primary chakra system). The chakra system and the human aura are directly connected to our emotions and self-patterning, or self-beliefs. We are what we think, and as we think our thoughts each day, they are projected into the aura, which flows with colours and energy.

The human aura is the flow of electro magnetic energy that surrounds each of us. We have all experienced feelings that emanate from the human aura. For instance, if someone stands too close to you, you may feel uncomfortable and feel as if the person is standing in your own personal space or aura.

In the human aura we have what are called star points. These star points allow the electro magnetic energy to move around the aura. Even though there are star points all around the human aura I will just concentrate on two of them: The universal star point and the earthing star point.

Universal Star Point

The Universal Star point is at the very top of the aura and is our connection to positive energy. The colour for the star point is pure white, and the energy that emanates from this point allows the flow of universal light to our crown chakra. The positive energy is then split throughout the human body like a prism, causing a rainbow effect upon the primary chakra system. The positive energy that flows from the universal star point allows the energy to flow through the primary chakra system via our kundalini – a line that flows and connects all chakra points, from the crown to the base.

Earthing Star Point

The next star point is the earth connection, which flows beneath our feet in the human aura. The Earthing Star point is our connection to the earth and its colour is silver. Human beings have very large chakra points on the bases of the feet and the earthing star point allows the energy of the earth to flow via these points into the body and assists in the release of energy to earth. The clearer the contact that we can have from positive to earth (from the universal star point to the earthing star point), the higher the vibration of the body and the healthier our mental attitude.

If our primary chakra system is closed down slightly on any one of the seven levels, this will cause a reduction in positive electrical flow, and a reduction in energy leading to stress and ill health. When we are fit and healthy and thinking positively about ourselves we flow with positive energy throughout our physical and electrical body.

If we find that we are stressed or worried, or find that we have suffered heartache through a loss or separation, we may find that we are drained on one or all levels of the primary chakra system. This will cause energy loss, which can cause sickness and ill health.

Because the human chakra system is located over the human spinal column and nervous system, if the energy is allowed to lower or become blocked for long periods of time, you will feel it as backache. Where the back aches tells you which chakra is lowered in energy.

Base Chakra

Colour: Red

The Base Chakra is connected to the Goddess and earth energy. Early civilisation worshipped the female Goddess as well as male Gods. The Goddess is connected to nurturing and the seasons, female energy, or Mother Earth.

The base chakra is directly connected to our loved ones and the position in which we place ourselves upon the earth. If we find that our values are threatened or lowered by the environment we will find that the base chakra is lowered in energy. This can lead to physical ill health of the sexual organs, anal problems, displacement of the hips and cause problems throughout the legs. The base chakra is our connection to the earth. It is connected to the roots we place upon the earth. If we have insecure roots, we suffer pain in our lower body.

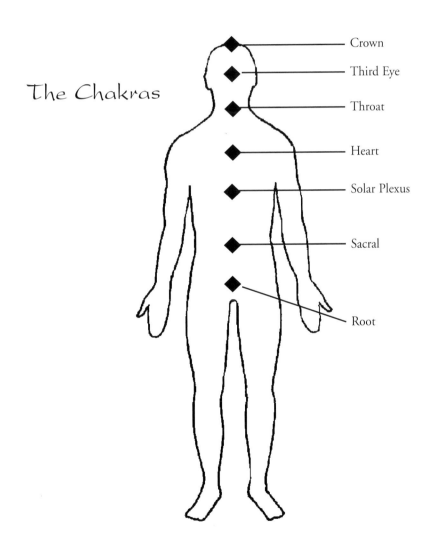

The Chakras

Crown

Third Eye

Throat

Heart

Solar Plexus

Sacral

Root

Sacral Chakra

Colour: Orange

The Sacral Chakra is connected to our instincts and is related to our Spirit Totems – the creature selves that we all possess. You have probably heard people describe others by saying things like: "He has the heart of a lion," "The strength of a bear," or "The eyes of an eagle". Primitive shamans wore the skin of their totem animal to encompass the energy or spirit of the animal so it could guide them on their spiritual journey.

Spirit totems rule the gut feelings we get when we are in danger. We cannot turn the radio on to find out what our spirit totems wish us to do today, but we can listen to our feelings. Your spirit totems are there to help keep you on your true path – they speak to you through instincts. If we fight them and do not listen to our gut feelings we could end up in trouble.

The sacral is related to our instinctive nature and our ability to listen to ourselves.

If we find that the environment is dictating to us in a way that stops us responding to our feelings we will find that our stomach will begin to feel as if it's in a knot. Listening to your gut feelings is listening to your instincts. If we carry on ignoring our true feelings we can inevitably find health problems effecting areas of our lower abdomen, small intestine, bowel, etc.

Solar Plexus Chakra

Colour: Yellow

The Solar Plexus Chakra is your eternal or divine spirit, which is the Godhead within. It is called the subconscious and super-conscious level, from where we get our intuition and visual thoughts. We are all divine, and have the ability to follow the eternal plan of our lives by following intuitive leads.

The subconscious and divine spirit levels of awareness are our clairvoyant self. The yellow chakra is our clairvoyant level and we are all clairvoyants. The Key to the Universe is within us and we are all connected to all things.

The solar plexus is directly associated to how and what we are thinking of ourselves.

If we are suffering from low self esteem, it is because we are in fear of making mistakes.

When we are confident, we don't fear making mistakes and even learn from our mistakes. If low self-esteem is allowed to persist we can find that all of the vital organs can be affected in one way or another.

Three Levels of Experience

In the beginning, when the Gods created the experience of the Universe there was only light: The light of absolute love and acceptance.

The Gods created the Universe and formed the light energy into life. Some energy is formless and divides the Universe into separate levels of existence – including the angel and astral levels. The astral level is the closest level to solid form and holds the realms of those that have recently passed over through death.

Since the beginning of time, creatures have to experience the lessons of life and challenges within the boundaries of their physical form and basic instinct. The Gods knew that the journey of life would be difficult for the human condition, and the light of man would wish to return to light. We all chose to experience the journey of life and in doing so we accepted the challenge of mortality.

We come from love and when we die we go to love.
We come from light and when we die we go to the light.

When the Gods created the Universe they where discussing where they should hide the keys to the Universe. Some Gods thought that the keys should be placed on the highest mountain. But the Gods realised that through time man would climb the highest mountains and find the keys. Some Gods thought that the keys should be hidden in the far reaches of the earth and be placed in the coldest places. But again they realised that through time man would explore and find them. Other Gods thought that the keys should be hidden in the deepest of oceans. Again, they realised that because of mans inquisitive nature he would find the keys.

After long discussions the Gods decided that they would hide the keys to the Universe within man, and give him three levels of awareness: The Divine Spirit or super conscious is the door to the Universe; the subconscious is the key to the Universe and the conscious is the experience of life.

Heart Chakra

Colour: Green

The Heart Chakra is connected to healing. Through the heart chakra we can all heal the environment with intention and thoughts. The energy of the Christ, Buddha and enlightened prophets all derive from the heart. Through this level of awareness comes our perception of the environment. The Prophets and all great spiritual persons that have lived throughout time have spoken from the heart about the way to live. They have all stated that the light is within everyone.

The heart generates love energy to the environment. If we do not love ourselves, we will find it hard to generate love to anyone else – unless the person in the environment accepts us for who we are and loves us for being us. Such unconditional love has the ability to open our heart, because we feel the love coming to us.

The yellow (solar plexus) and the green chakra points are directly connected to our emotions. We hold our personal lessons in the yellow chakra and how we feel towards others in the environment in our green chakra.

For example

If we feel that we are insecure, have issues of low self-esteem, or act negatively towards others in the environment we feel it on a personal level. In other words it's how we react and feel towards others that creates the atmosphere of the environment. If we have suffered from rejection from a loved one or sustained a loss we feel it in our heart, in the form of heartache. How we feel towards others is reflected back at us in the form of our lessons.

You can only love others as much as you love yourself. You can only accept others as much as you accept yourself. How you feel towards yourself is directly proportional to how you react with others. Lessons will come to us directly proportional to the feeling and energy that we hold for ourselves.

Issues of insecurity, low self esteem and negativity come from fearing lessons. Security, confidence, and positively towards others comes from learning from your lessons. No one is perfect and we are all here to learn our lessons. If we had no lessons to learn we would all walk and talk from the time we were born. However we are all going to fall flat on our backsides at least once in our lives.

The yellow and green chakra points are also directly connected to the etheric level of the human aura system. The etheric level of the human aura is the third and fourth level of aura and is responsible for human emotions. It is located approximately two inches from the human physical body and is an excellent location to place your hands over a client during a healing. You can perform a total healing this way, without physically touching a client. This form of healing will help balance any emotional problems. The etheric level can be seen on early paintings of the Christ and saints as a halo.

If we hold issues of negativity in our yellow chakra, this flows out through our green or heart chakra and into the aura. This tells others in the environment that you have issues of negativity or low self esteem, because they will feel it in the form of emotions coming from you and will react accordingly. This is turn alters the energy of the environment that surrounds you. We have all suffered from insecurity, low self esteem or reacted negatively towards others in the environment at least once in our lives.

The environment is like a living mirror that holds the lesson that we need to overcome. Once we have learned to love and accept ourselves as we are, and let go of the issues that are connecting us to the lesson we can become positive within our environment.

Throat Chakra

Colour: Blue

The Throat Chakra is connected to communication and is the realm of the angels. The way we talk to each other creates energy directed to the environment. If we talk negatively to the environment or talk about people negatively we will create negative experiences.

For example

Let's say that we have a problem with someone, they have hurt us emotionally, not accepted us as we are, and seem to be passive aggressive. This means that they are nice to us one moment and negative to us the next, causing us to feel insecure and threatened. We have been hurt and the energy of the situation is causing us to think deep thoughts. Our colours are dark and we don't know how to handle the situation.

We talk to people we feel we can trust, to the detriment of the person that shows passive aggressive behaviour towards us. Using words negatively will create negative situations for us in the environment. It really does us no good to express negativity outside of the situation to others. We may feel that we have released the situation by talking to others about the problem – but it is just a slight and temporary release of our feelings.

In truth the passive aggressive is getting what they want – for you to give them your energy. When we are talking, or thinking of others we are giving them our energy. This can be used positively. We all have the ability to heal others and ourselves by the use of intention and strength of our words.

There is another way to deal with such a situation: See the passive aggressive as a person who has been very hurt as a child. See them only as a child with a very poor attitude towards life and others. The younger you can see the child the better. Imagine giving the child the discipline, love and acceptance that they didn't receive when they where growing up. Talk to the child with the use of your thoughts.

This will give you the ability to have compassion and understanding when you next meet the passive aggressive person. In your minds eye keep them as a child and your subconscious will give you the answers you are looking for. Most of the problems with adults were created as children.

As you discuss your feelings with the passive aggressive you are also discussing your feelings with yourself. Showing compassion and understanding to the passive aggressive person shows compassion and understanding to you, too.

If we cannot resolve our issues with communication and by discussing our desires, wishes and needs we don't have a positive relationship with others or ourselves. To talk clearly and from the heart is to talk your truth. People can experience blockages in the throat chakra as coughs, sore throats, a weakened voice, or the feeling that there is something stuck in the throat.

Life and death are in the power of the tongue so be very careful of what you say and the way you say things. Words create energy and we all have the ability to manifest our life. (How about 'Words have energy and we all create our own life.') If you are saying negative things with determination into the environment you are determined to bring negativity to you. Do not talk about others negatively because by doing so you are focusing on the negative aspect of yourself.

If we hold on to our words and fear expressing our opinion we have to look at why we feel this way. We can only talk from our hearts and in honesty of our true feelings. If you do not speak openly your health can be affected in the throat and lungs region. Tension in the throat chakra can also cause anxiety attacks.

The Angel Realms

The angels communicate with us to bring change to mankind. We all have a host of angels to protect us and keep us from harm. The angels communicate to us in the form of our feelings. We have the freedom of choice and free will to live this life and experience it in whatever form we please. The angels cannot and will not interfere with our freedom of choice and free will.

We all have a personal angel and it is the divine duty of the personal angel to watch over us. It doesn't matter what we do or say, the personal angel is compassionate and understands us as we are.

Our angel sees us as light and knows our lesson in life and what we have to overcome. We are all born with limited knowledge, and experience life with limitations. We all make mistakes and are here to learn. As we go through life, we sometimes get stuck in a rut or a lesson and find ourselves going around in circles. We may pray or use affirmations, which can help us through certain situations. We have the freedom of choice and will not get help unless we ask for it.

"Ask and thy will receive".

You must ask the question before the angels can start to create positive change for you. Your personal angel will be delighted to see that you no longer wish to fumble around in the dark. This will cause the personal angel to react and call upon your archangels, who are there to release negativity out of your environment. The archangels purpose is to take you from light to light – in other words, allow you to follow the divine plan of your life. The archangels are totally selfish (selfish?) on your behalf and are only interested in the divine plan of your life.

Third Eye / Brow Chakra

Colour: Indigo

The Indigo Chakra is our third eye or pituitary gland. Our third eye is connected to our thoughts and the Highest Guide of the Light. The purpose of this guidance is to take us to the light with the use of our thoughts and intuition on a conscious level. It is our route to enlightenment.

We generate energy with our thoughts in the form of feelings. These feelings flow through our primary chakra system to the aura and create the experience of life. If our thoughts are in harmony with the environment we are balanced and in harmony with ourselves.

We think through the use of our conscious state in the form of pictures and mental images, either with our eyes closed or open. (?) When we think of situations that occurred in our past we draw in the energy of the time and place it within our aura. The inner healer will help you overcome your karma if you state your intention to heal the past.

The third eye is directly associated to our thoughts – what we are thinking of ourselves and our position in our environment. If we persist in thinking negatively about our lives and the environment we must start looking at why this is. There will always be others better than you and there will always be others worse off than you. Changing your perception of the environment will allow you to change the perception of your self. Negative thinking causes migraines, tension headaches, neck problems, and obstructs the energy flow throughout the whole of the primary chakra system.

Crown Chakra

Colour: Violet

The Crown Chakra is connected to our true self – our higher self. It is our connection to the Universal light. God, Allah, whatever different cultures have called the highest light, it is the energy we possess through the realm of the crown chakra.

This is the pure positive light of unconditional love and acceptance, which is then split into every colour of the rainbow through your chakra system, starting from the crown chakra and flowing to your base red chakra, through the kundalini.

We all have Highest Guides of Universal Light. They are our Sherpas – guiding us up our mountain called life. The guides are there to give us healing and messages so we can bring spiritual growth into our lives. The Highest Guides of Universal Light may change constantly as we develop through our life. We may access lots of guides to help us with different issues and lessons, or we may have one dominant guide who is capable of handling every issue faced through life. However, this is rare and all Universal Guides are responsible for your divine guidance. They will access the inner growth and bring positive change into your life.

The crown chakra is directly associated to how connected we are to ourselves: "The inner divine connected to the outer divine".

If we feel that we are disconnected from the environment we can start to feel depressed and alone, angry, frustrated and resentful. The energy of the universe is unconditional. The truth is you are putting conditions on your love. Love yourself unconditionally. You are here because God wishes you to be here. Accept the Divinity that you are and connect to the love of the universe by simple accepting who you are. This will connect you to the Divine light, which is Universal.

The Dai,Ko,Myo, is the closest Reiki symbol to connect you with the Universal Light, it will attune you to the Universe and bring spiritual growth into your life.

Chapter 3

The Reiki Ideals

The Reiki ideals are a set of rules that will help you to access a happier, more fulfilled and less complicated life. They can also help to explain the human condition and how we as humans are affected by the environment and can suffer energy loss.

Just for today, I will let go of anger.

Just for today, I will let go of worry.

Just for today, I will give thanks for my many blessings.

Just for today, I will do my work honestly.

Just for today, I will be kind to my neighbour and every living thing.

These ideals are very easy to read but what do they mean? And how can you truly place these ideals into your life? For example, how do you get rid of anger when your mother in law keeps interfering in your life? How are you going to stop worrying when your life is falling apart, and you are going to lose your job/partner/home? Let's look at each one in turn.

Just for today, I will let go of anger.

To understand anger we have to look at why we feel angry. In truth, you are not really angry with anyone else – you are only angry with yourself, for allowing the situation to happen in the first place. Anger is also the second stage of fear – there cannot be anger without fear preceding it.

Anger is an internal state that you project out onto the world – just as love is.

Have you ever been in love with someone? You have connected to someone and through this connection you are flowing with positive energy or love. You value this person and feel wonderful that this person actually likes you for you. You feel loved and accepted. Even when you are separate from this person, your thoughts flow to each other and you both think the experience is wonderful.

When you are experiencing such love, it is as if the world has a golden glow around it. Suddenly you see other people holding hands and glowing, too, and the world seems wonderful. It is as if the whole world is in love.

On the other side of the coin, have you ever felt angry with someone and then felt as if the whole world is out to get you? You wake up in a bad mood and feel terrible. You have a bad back and the last thing you feel like is going to work. You spill coffee down you. You have difficulty starting the car and on the way to work every traffic light is on red, making you late and irritable. Everyone seems to be driving aggressively and it's as if every driver on the road is out to abuse you. Welcome to cause and effect. What we say and do creates energy.

Be aware of what you say and do, because what you say and do to others will happen to you. When we are in love we are showing care and forgiveness towards others, this creates an environment of care and forgiveness. When we are in a bad mood we get irritable and the world gets irritable back.

If we find that what we value and love is being threatened by others in the environment we are not truly valuing ourselves. Anger is a form of protection to release us from negative situations that occur in our lives. To understand anger you have to understand why we get angry in the first place. To live in anger for long periods of time can cause illness and dis-ease. Source what is wrong with your environment and recognise where you are not getting valued and why. Value yourself as yourself. If others cannot accept you, that's their problem.

Just for today, I will let go of worry.

When we are worried we are trying too hard. We are putting our own energy into the situation, and on certain levels draining ourselves. If we worry for long periods of time we find that our health will be reduced and pain arises through certain parts of our body. The question has to be asked, why do we worry?

We worry when we are not accepted or loved by the people in our environment; we feel as if we are losing control of our environment and the Universe that we have created around us.

Imagine driving to work and leaving your lights on when you get to your destination. The car engine has stopped and there is no back up power or generator to supply the battery – the lights will dim and die. When you are worried you are relying on the human battery – the chakra system – to supply electricity to energise the lights of your mind.

In a very short period of time you will find that the battery is flat and holds no power. When we worry we are draining our own battery, in a sense leaving our lights on. We think of situations that worry us, 24 hour a day – when awake, asleep, when we talk to friends. Why do we do this?

The human consciousness tries to control our environment and we search for love and acceptance. Yet in truth we do not have to search. Divine love and perfect health are our true form of existence and we are all one. All is connected.

If we try to control the environment we will be controlled. If we try to fight the environment, people will fight back and be confrontational. Our environment is a direct reflection of us. This is where our lessons come to our level of existence.

How does this work?

When you are worried you are thinking of the person or situation. When you are thinking of the situation you are putting your energy towards the area that you are focusing upon, with the strength of your mind. You create more and more worry.

For example, imagine a situation where you are worried about a person who is doing the wrong thing to you – possibly you have had an argument or they are controlling you. You are worried because you don't really know how to overcome the situation.

Your subconscious doesn't only think of the current situation, but starts to bring up other situations that have happened throughout your life: things that happened last week, last year, ten years ago, when you where five years old. In fact the subconscious brings everything out of the library of life that is similar to this situation. Suddenly your worry is magnified. Worry is energy that can be better used, so redirect your thoughts.

Just for today, I will give thanks for my many blessings.

We are all born into the world fully equipped to fulfil our destiny and complete our life lesson. There is nothing that you need that you do not all ready have. Nothing is achieved by wanting. Nothing is achieved by placing responsibility to a higher authority – in other words, blaming others for your situation. Belief is the act of living.

We all believe in something, even if you're an atheist you believe in something that is nothing. The human will is the medium to the soul. This is the root to the knowledge. This is the root to the personal God because God is within us all. This is the "I" in " I am, that I am."

—An interpretation of the words of Jehovah

Christ said, "The Christ is within us all".

Budda said, "Budda is within us all".

And the light of God is within all of us.

To be focusing on wanting, is focusing on lack instead of focusing on what you already have. We are all born in the form of God with unique gifts and tools and our own special qualities. We all have very many blessings.

The Universe is God split into a billion particles and we all create our own Universe with the use of our thoughts and perceptions. We are all born with the freedom of choice and free will and nothing can take this away from us.

You may base your belief on the amount of wealth that you own, or the area that you live in, and say, "I am doing okay in the world because I have lots of stuff." Remember, we are born with nothing, and when we die, we leave with nothing.

The only thing we truly own is within us – our thoughts and feelings we carry for eternity.

Our thoughts and feelings create our life through karma. What we thought of five years ago created what happened four years ago. What you thought of last year, created this year. What you did last week, created this week and what you do today, will create your tomorrow. We have the ability to create miracles, if it is part of our divine plan.

We all have a divine plan. To follow a plan that is not part of your divine plan will create sadness and unhappy situations because you are trying to play God – possibly hurting others through your determination to have control and power.

We are all born from love and when we die we go to love. The Universal light is the energy of total unconditional love and acceptance. In other words it loves and accepts you, no matter what you have done through life. Through the journey of life you are sourcing love and acceptance. Love is the most powerful of all the energy processes and to accept others unconditionally is to start to follow the divine plan of your life.

The Universe was created through unbalance, and as the Universe is expanding we have to expand and grow with it. The Cosmos and the Planets are slightly imperfect and so are we. If you look at a rose you may see a perfect flower. But when you look close you can see the imperfections that make the rose perfect. In the eyes of God, we are all similar to the rose. We all have imperfections and we are all unique. Accept that you are not perfect, the environment is not perfect, and everyone in it is not perfect. To look for perfection within your self can only lead to dissatisfaction.

We try to be perfect, and if one person doesn't accept us for who we are, we focus on the reasons why we are not loved and accepted. We can get angry, frustrated, or fall into fear and depression, because we are imperfect. The human condition means we are all imperfect. Love what and who you are. To get angry or fearful is to be none accepting of your divine path. This will divert you off your path until you accept, or clear the situation in your own mind.

Your environment is a reflection of you. You get back what you give out. To speak or act negative to another, will create negative karma for you. To go looking for total love and acceptance from others in an un-perfect cosmos, will give you a lesson in love and acceptance. We are all here for lessons.

Accept others as yourself; to fight another is to fight you.

Accept yourself and accept your imperfections.

Replace fear with love and compassion and follow the divine plan of your life.

There is nothing you need that you do not already have. Give thanks for your many blessings, because there will always be people you consider better off than you, and others worse off than you. Accept that you are only human. We all have faults. Concentrate on your many blessings – you get more of what you focus on.

Just for today, I will do my work honestly.

This speaks for itself. Being honest means taking responsibility. We all have a responsibility to live this life, and be true to ourselves. In the words of William Shakespeare: "To thy own self be true".

We can endeavour to live our life in a way that fulfils other people's expectations of us. We are all part of the environment and some times the environment – and the people in it – dictates to us what we have to do throughout our lives. We can get ill or stressed because we feel we have to follow the divine plan of others before we can follow our own. In this situation we are being drained of our energy and controlled negatively. We are all controlled to a degree by governments or the price of food that we buy, but we all have freedom of choice and free will, to live our lives the way we choose. Sometimes it is only our perception we have to change to alter the situation.

To be in full battle dress and fight the situation will fuel the fire and cause conflict.

I am not saying that you have to cower in a corner, or hope that God will sort all of your situations out for you. I am saying that we were given a voice, and the ability to communicate. If you speak your truths from the heart they will put you in line with your destiny. If people start getting angry at your truth, they do not value you. Be totally honest with yourself about how you wish to use the currency of your life.

We all have the choice of what we accept and reject. If people are hurting your feelings, you don't have to accept this. No one has the right to hurt another, abuse another or invade another's personal boundaries. Feelings are your power.

To suppress your feeling is to suppress you.

No matter what you have done through your life, you have lived your life the best way you can with the limited knowledge you have had at any one time. We are all wounded, and we carry these wounds through life. From my experience it doesn't matter if you where abused physically, sexually, mentally or shouted at once in your entire childhood – the experience was hurtful to you.

We chose our lessons and life experiences and we chose to be where we are right now. This place is where we are meant to be. Whether you are a top class lawyer, doctor, or a prisoner in gaol you are where you are meant to be. Do not resist the situation of where you are. Do not blame others for your circumstances. You have created them. And you can take responsibility to better the situation you are in, by loving yourself and being honest with yourself.

Just for today, I will be kind to my neighbour and every living thing.

Everything in life has purpose and meaning, from the smallest of creatures, to the largest seas. We are all connected to all things and what we say or do affects everything.

The mind is like a magnet that attracts situations into our reality. Imagine you are thinking of someone you haven't seen for years, and then out of the blue there they are – walking down the street, calling upon your house, or phoning you. Every thought you have makes a difference.

We are all clairvoyants and we all have the ability to heal others and ourselves.

We are Universal with a Universal consciousness, what we think and do in the environment creates the illusion of life. We are moving through the Cosmos at a fantastic rate, and as the Universe is moving we must move with our awareness in order to keep up.

If you talk negatively about another person you are calling yourself, if you despise another, you despise a part of yourself. The environment is a mirror image of you.

What you need to learn will come to you from the environment.

We all 'feel' situations and the energy people give off when they are talking to us. Sometimes you hear one thing and feel another – because you can sense the truth behind the words. We all have feelings, however in Western society our feelings are the first thing we are taught to ignore, because they hurt. How many times have you been told not to cry, or respond to painful situations? From an early age we are taught to hold our emotions in, and this creates pain.

Life force is the energy that is given off by all life, including you. To experience life force is to experience the feel of the environment: the trees, bees, birds, animals and everything in it. Feeling is so important to us, it is our intuition.

The Cosmos also gives off life force energy. Astrology is the science of how the Cosmos effects our lives – how this energy affects our moods and emotions. The Moon affects certain situations and is a very powerful energy source in itself. Our bodies are composed of seventy percent water and since the Moon affects the oceans, it makes sense that our emotions are not immune to its effects and cycles.

We are given sign posts throughout our lives that are there to help us in our lives.

This is an art in itself – to recognise these signs and to remain aware at all times. If a butterfly flies close to us, or we see a dolphin, or a fox, however large or small, common or rare –

they are all animal totems. This is very much a shamanistic process, and we are all shamans. Shamans are people that follow their spiritual path.

We all dream and we are all spiritual creatures that are evolving in the Cosmos.

We are all part of the Universe, every living thing is connected. Showing kindness to all living things is showing kindness to you. If you are not feeling like showing kindness to others then ask yourself why you are feeling this way about yourself? See it as a lesson for you and resist creating further karma by being unkind. Break the cycle and love yourself.

Chapter 4

Reiki Level III

The Steps to Self-Attune with the Symbols of Reiki

First of all please read these instructions through before starting with the exercises. As mentioned earlier, I also recommend that you read the book through once before doing any of the exercises. The reason for reading the book first is to release the information first to your subconscious level and higher self. This will prepare you for the Reiki symbols to be aligned to your inner vibration.

Follow each exercise with your eyes open. Once you have completed each exercise in the book with your eyes open, go back and repeat each exercise in turn with your eyes closed, where appropriate.

Carefully follow the step-by-step directions to attune your self to the Reiki symbols – don't miss any out. As you attune yourself acknowledge your feelings and subtle shifts in energy as the symbols become attuned to your inner vibration.

If you find that you have gone into a feeling of deep trance as you go through the attuning process, please acknowledge that all is well. Reiki is a healing process and all you have experienced is the healing qualities of the symbols as they align themselves with your inner vibration.

The responsibility to fully complete the attuning process falls upon you as an individual. Some may complete the book in a few hours, and others a week, or weeks.

If you wish to go over the attuning process more than once, continually aligning yourself with the symbols over a period of time, then please do so. This is not a necessity, but if you feel the need for reinforcement then it will be beneficial to you.

As you attune yourself to the symbols of Reiki you will find the reasons why you where originally attracted to this book. We all experience lessons in our own way, and this book allows you to experience attuning yourself to Reiki symbols in your own time, at your own level, while capturing your own unique qualities.

While you are going through the steps of attuning the symbols to your vibration, you may find that your mind cannot seem to focus on the direction of the steps you have been given to follow. Please accept that the symbol is still attuning to your vibration. Through time the symbols will help you to focus. Even if you find that you fall asleep during the process of going through the book, accept the symbol is still attuning itself to your vibration as you rest.

With each step there is a recommended time period given to attune you. However, if you are slightly over or under the time period given do not worry. It is only a recommended time and you may feel that you need more time or less time to go through each step. Do what you feel is necessary.

Acknowledge your feelings as you go through the book. Reiki works on the electrical vibration of the human body, which is directly connected to your emotions. If you find that your mind is beginning to wander, please acknowledge that you are probably releasing negative emotions connected to your thoughts and feelings.

If while going through the book you find yourself sitting in an uncomfortable position, then please move and adjust yourself so that you are comfortable. This is your book and your time, so please enjoy the experience.

I am going to show you how to attune yourself to the symbols of Reiki by positioning your hands over certain parts of your body and using the strength of your breath. Your breath is the key to your health. It is written that when God created the earth he brought the wind to bring changes throughout the planet. Your breath is the wind that changes you within. When we are anxious we sigh and breathe deeper than normal. When we are stressed we breathe short breaths. By using the strength of your breath you will align the symbols to your vibration and connect to the energy of the symbol.

Hands-on healing is as old as the hills. When we hurt ourselves we naturally cover the pain with our hands and when our children hurt themselves we cover their pain with our hands. There is nothing new about hands-on healing – we have used it since time began. This book will help you explore why we do these things. It is intended to align you with the healing energy that we all posses, so you can be a stronger person on the physical, mental, emotional and spiritual level.

Step One

State your intention to attune yourself to the seven sacred symbols of Reiki.

Say these words, either out loud or to yourself:

I call upon the light of the Universe to enter this place as divine love and spiritual guidance.

I pray for you to cleanse me as a healer of light.

I wish to attune myself to the seven symbols of Reiki and align myself to the energy of each symbol.

I invoke the energy of my Reiki guide and teacher, to guide me through life, so I can heal my life, my environment, and myself.

May the Universal life force energy that is Reiki flow through me and lead me to the right way of feeling and living my life.

Amen.

Step Two

Sit comfortably upon the floor with your legs crossed, or sit upon a chair with your feet placed flat upon the floor.

Place your hands flat upon the floor at either side of you with your palms facing downwards. Close your eyes.

Breathe in through your nose and out through your mouth.

Imagine taking the breath all the way down through your body: Your neck, shoulders, arms, stomach, hips, thighs, knees, calves, and all the way to your feet. Do this for four minutes.

Now imagine a silver cord flowing out from the palms of your hands and the base of your spine, flowing down deep into the Earth. Do this for four minutes.

Open your eyes.

This exercise will connect you to the energy of the earth. Even if you do not experience anything different at this point in time, please accept the fact that you have stated your intention to connect to the energy of the Earth, and know that higher realms will clear the path for you.

Step Three

1. Close your eyes and imagine a ball of light about a metre above the top of your head.

2. Imagine beams of light flowing down from this ball of light all around you.

3. In your minds eye imagine yourself in a crystal ball – filling it with light. Concentrate upon this for four minutes.

4. Now imagine this light flowing in through the top of your head through your crown chakra (your crown chakra is located where your soft spot was when you where first born).

5. Imagine this light flowing through your body. Down through your head, your shoulders, your arms. Through your chest, stomach, hips, thighs, knees, calves, ankles and out through your feet to combine with the light flowing around you.

6. Concentrate for four minutes.

This will connect you to the energy of the Universal light. This is the light of unconditional love and acceptance. When we are born into the World we expect unconditional love and acceptance from our parents and those around us. As we develop through life we have conditions placed upon us by our parents and our environment. By the time we mature to adults we learn to place conditions on others for our love and acceptance, and the cycle continues from adult to child.

The Universe understands the lessons that you have chosen to learn through all lives. You have Universal qualities within you and the Universe will help you, all you have to do is ask for help.

Step Four

1. Please read the information first and look at the pictures provided to get an idea where to place your hands.

2. Focus upon the symbol of DAI KO MYO and endeavour to associate the symbol to something you can recognize in every day life. For example, possibly the symbol may look like a snail, shell or a musical note. This will help you remember and recall the symbol. It will familiarise your conscious mind with the symbol, and prepare the subconscious mind to accept the energy of the DAI KO MYO.

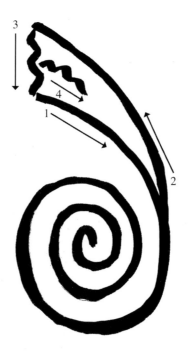

The DAI KO MYO.

Means: The desire for enlightenment.

To be one with the Goddess

Used to heal depreciating personal values

3. Follow the arrows given with the Symbol to show you how to draw the DAI KO MYO with your fingers.

4. Once you are confident that you can draw the symbol with your fingers, close your eyes and draw the symbol onto the air in front of you.

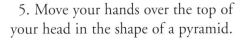

5. Move your hands over the top of your head in the shape of a pyramid.

6. Place one hand over your groin and the other over your forehead

7. Breathe in through your nose, and imagine taking the breath all the way to your lower hand covering your groin. Take the breath out through your mouth. The breathing technique will align the symbol to your inner vibration. Do this for four minutes. Make sure your eyes are closed while you are aligning the symbol to your vibration to help you feel the subtle shifts in energy.

8. Connect to the Inner Goddess.

Step Five

1. Please read the instructions first and look at the pictures provided to get an idea of where to place your hands.

2. Focus upon the symbol of the HON SHA ZE SHO NEN and endeavor to associate the symbol to something that you can recognise from every-day life. For example a tree or a tower block. This will help you remember and recall the symbol. It will familiarise your conscious mind with the symbol and prepare your subconscious mind to accept the energy of the HON SHA ZE SHO NEN.

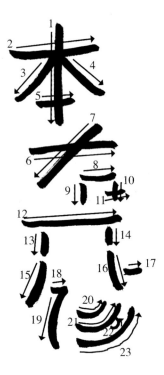

The HON SHA ZE SHO NEN.

Means: No past. No present. No future.

It is used to heal Karma.

3. Follow the arrows given with the symbol to show you how to draw the HON SHA ZE SHO NEN with your fingers.

4. Once you are confident that you can draw the symbol with you fingers, close your eyes and draw the symbol onto the air in front of you.

5. Move your hands over your head in the shape of a pyramid.

6. Place one hand over your lower abdomen and the other hand over your forehead.

7. Breathe in through your nose, and imagine taking the breath all the way to your lower hand covering your lower abdomen. Take the breath out through your mouth. This breathing technique will connect you to the symbol. Do this breathing exercise for a few minutes. Make sure your eyes are closed while performing the breathing exercise.

8. Listen to your instincts.

Step Six

1. Please read the information first and look at the pictures provided to get an idea of where to place your hands.

2. Focus upon the symbol of the CHO KU REI and endeavor to associate the symbol to something you can recognize in every day life. For example a music note, or a shell. This will help you remember and recall the symbol. It will familiarize your conscious mind with the symbol and prepare the sub conscious mind to accept the energy of the CHO KU REI.

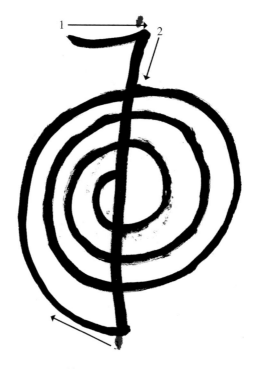

The CHO KU REI

Means: to increase the power of the divine self

Used to increase energy and for empowering the self.

Also used to heal negative personal issues,

such as low self esteem and lack of self-confidence.

3. Follow the arrows given to show you how to draw the symbol with your fingers.

4. Once you are confident that you can draw the symbol with your fingers, close your eyes and draw the symbol onto the air in front of you.

5. Place your hands over the top of your head in the shape of a pyramid.

6. Place one hand three to four fingers above your belly button and the other hand over your forehead.

7. Breathe in through your nose, and imagine taking the breath all the way to your lower hand above your belly button. Take the breath out through your mouth. This breathing technique will connect you to the symbol. Do this breathing exercise for four minutes. Please close your eyes while performing the attuning process.

8. Feel the Divine that is within.

Step Seven

1. Please read the information first and look at the pictures provided to get an idea where to place your hands.

   Note: There are two CHO-KU-REI symbols one is left and the other is right.

2. Focus upon the symbol of CHO KU REI and endeavor to associate the symbol to something you can recognize in every day life. For example, possibly the symbol may look like a snail, shell or a musical note. This will help you recall and remember the symbol. It will familiarize your conscious mind with the symbol and prepare the subconscious mind to accept the energy of the CHO KU REI.

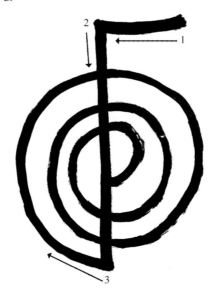

The CHO KU REI.

Means: to be one with the divine environment.

To be one with the Christ.

Used to increase energy and release negativity related to environmental issues.

3. Follow the arrows given with the symbol to show you how to draw the CHO KU REI with your fingers.

4. Once you are confident that you can draw the symbol with your fingers, close your eyes and draw the symbol onto the air in front of you.

5. Move your hands over the top of your head in the shape of a pyramid.

6. Place one hand over your heart and the other hand over your forehead.

7. Breathe in through your nose, and imagine taking the breath all the way to your lower hand covering your heart. Take the breath out through your mouth. This breathing technique will connect you to the symbol. Do this breathing exercise for four minutes.

8. Feel the love of Christ become your love.

Step Eight

1. Please read the information first and look at the pictures provided to get an idea where to place your hands.

2. Focus upon the symbol of SEI HE KI and endeavor to associate the symbol to something you can recognize in every day life. For example, possibly the symbol may look like a horse, person or an animal. This will help you remember and recall the symbol. It will familiarize your conscious mind with the symbol and prepare the subconscious mind to accept the energy of the SEI HE KI.

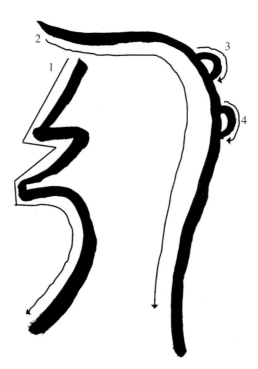

The SEI HE KI.

Means: to communicate with love.

To be one with the angels.

To be used to heal negative issues related to communication.

3. Follow the arrows given with the symbol to show you how to draw the SEI HE KI with your fingers.

4. Once you are confident that you can draw the symbol with your fingers, close your eyes and draw the symbol onto the air in front of you.

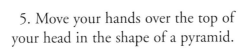

5. Move your hands over the top of your head in the shape of a pyramid.

6. Place one hand over your throat and the other over your forehead.

7. Breathe in through your nose, and imagine taking the breath all the way to your lower hand covering your throat. Take the breath out through your mouth. This breathing technique will connect you to the symbol. Do this breathing exercise for four minutes.

8. Feel the energy of your angel.

Step Nine

1. Please read the information first and look at the pictures provided to get an idea where to place your hands.

2. Focus upon the symbol of RAKU and endeavor to associate the symbol to something you can recognise in every day life. For example, possibly the symbol may look like a lightening bolt. This will help you remember and recall the symbol. It will familiarise your conscious mind with the symbol and prepare the subconscious mind to accept the energy of the RAKU.

The RAKU.

Means: to align the Universe to Earth.

To be one with Reiki Healing energy.

To be used to heal issues related to negative thinking.

3. Follow the arrows given with the symbol to show you how to draw the RAKU with your fingers.

4. Once you are confident that you can draw the symbol with your fingers, close your eyes and draw the symbol onto the air in front of you.

5. Move your hands over the top of your head in the shape of a pyramid.

6. Place both hands over your eyes, with your fingers touching your third eye.

7. Breathe in through your nose, and imagine taking the breath all the way to your base chakra. Take the breath out through your mouth. This breathing technique will connect you to the symbol. Do this for four minutes.

8. Feel the symbol align the healing energy to your vibration.

Step Ten

1. Please read the information first and looks at the pictures provided to get an idea where to place your hands.

2. Focus upon the symbol of DAI KO MYO and endeavor to associate the symbol to something you can recognise in every day life. For example, possibly the symbol may look like a snail, shell or a musical note. This will help you remember and recall the symbol. It will familiarise your conscious mind to the symbol and prepare the subconscious mind to accept the energy of the DAI KO MYO.

The DAI KO MYO.

Means: to make oneself whole.

To be one with the Universe

Used to heal issues of disconnection and depression

3. Follow the arrows given with the symbol to show you how to draw the DAI KO MYO with your fingers.

4. Once you are confident that you can draw the symbol with your fingers, close your eyes and draw the symbol onto the air in front of you.

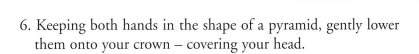

5. Move your hands over the top of your head in the shape of a pyramid.

6. Keeping both hands in the shape of a pyramid, gently lower them onto your crown – covering your head.

7. Breathe in through your nose, and imagine taking the breath all the way to your base chakra. Take the breath out through your mouth. This breathing technique will connect you to the symbol. Do this breathing technique for four minutes.

8. Feel the Reiki Guide of Love and Light become your light.

Chapter 5

Reiki Level II

Distance Healing

Reiki level two is distance healing, through the use of our thoughts. You can use a photograph or mental imagery to create a healing format.

We heal with the Principle of Intention to heal and the realisation that we are all connected. We don't have to be physically holding a client to heal them. We can heal others and ourselves with the use of our thoughts, at any distance.

Reiki level two is the use of symbols to create a healing format to release blocked energy. The self-attuning process and symbols will give you the ability to use Reiki level two as a healing format. This will give you the ability to practice Reiki on a continual basis and see the positive affects Reiki will give you to help you heal your life.

First of all check the list of symbols that you used through the attuning process. Traditionally you only use four symbols with distance healing:

Hon,Sha,Ze,Sho,Nen, to clear past and karmic issues.

Cho,Ku,Rei yellow and Cho,Ku,Rei green to enhance the healing format between the yellow and green chakra, which is directly connected to clearing emotional problems.

She,He,Ki, to release any communication problems and any retained energy through lack of communication.

However, I personally use all seven symbols to distance heal with great effect. I can see nothing wrong in using all seven symbols

Step One – using a photograph

This section of distance healing is the first process to help understand how we can use these techniques to assist in healing.

Take a look at a photograph of someone that you wish to heal. Concentrate upon the photo image for a few minutes.

Allow the self-attuning process and knowledge of the Reiki symbols to help you develop a healing format. The Reiki symbols are healing symbols; allow the symbols to flow between you and the photo with the use of your mind, thoughts and intention to heal.

Close your eyes and observe which symbols or symbol flow between your mind and the photo.

If you find this difficult you can use the Hon Sha Ze Sho Nen, the Shi He Ki, and the Cho Ku Rei yellow and Cho-Ku-Rei green to perform a healing format. Look at the photo and draw the symbols over the photo with your finger. This sequence of symbols will clear any negative issues from the person you desire to heal.

Step Two – distance healing using mental imaging

Think of a person that you wish to heal. Get a mental image of them in your mind, or a feeling of them if you are a less visual person.

Imagine the Reiki symbols flowing between you and the person that you wish to heal. Notice the way the symbols are flowing towards the person you wish to heal. Some symbols may be larger that others, telling you that some issues are larger than other issues. If the symbols flow in uniform sequence from your subconscious, this will tell you that the healing format is balanced. Observe in which sequence the symbols flow between you and the person you wish to heal.

If you find the Dai,Ko,Myo, or the Raku come into the sequence, observe the sequence that they come through. The Dai,Ko,Myo, is the connection to the earth or the Universe and if it shows in the sequence, this means that the person you desire to heal will be connected through this level and all negativity will be dissolved between the Earth or the Universe. If the Raku shows in the sequence of symbols, observe where the Raku enters the sequence. The Raku is the energy of alignment and is connected to the third eye. This symbol will align the healing energy so any negativity can be cleared.

If you find this technique difficult, you can still use the symbols by drawing them into the air to create a healing force. Life force energy is Pranic energy, which flows all around us. Pranic energy is life force in action and will carry the intention to the person that you wish to heal – whether you imagine the symbols, see them flow or draw them in the air.

Draw the Sei, He, Ki, and the Cho,Ku,Rei yellow and Cho-Ku-Rei green twice, and finish of with the Hon,Sha,Ze,Sho,Nen, to release any karmic issues the person you desire to heal may have.

Step Three – distance healing method to heal ourselves

Here we look at using distance healing to release any stressful issues that may be affecting us throughout our lives and help heal any past influence that is affecting the current situation.

Think of any issues that you are currently worried or stressed about. As you think of these issues, hold them in your imagination and imagine the Reiki symbols flowing between you and them. Observe the sequence of symbols that flow between you and the issues. With this technique you are effectively healing your past with the use of Reiki. You can do this with any situation in your past, however long ago it occurred.

If you find visualising the issue and the symbols difficult, think of the issue and draw the symbols with your hands in the air in front of you:

- She,He,Ki to release any communication problems.
- Cho,Ku,Rei yellow and green to release any emotional problems.
- Hon,Sha,Ze,Sho,Nen, to release any karmic issues.
- Raku, to align the energy to be released. (This will earth the situation and dissolve any negative issues into nothing).

Reiki level two is used to heal with the Universal law of intention. Once you state your intention to heal others or yourself the healing process is almost immediate. Reiki works the way it is meant to. It will flow to areas that need attending to first. Always remember we attract people into our lives that have similar issues to us – so whenever we heal others we are also healing ourselves.

To heal another is to heal our self.

To teach another is to be taught.

To counsel another is to be counselled.

Listen to what you say to others, because you are really saying it to yourself.

Chapter 6

Reiki Level 1

Healing the Physical Body with Your Hands

Humans have an ability to heal themselves and others with their hands. We do this instinctively when we hurt ourselves by covering the pain with our hands. If I were to bang my head I would instinctively cover the area that was painful with the palms of my hands. When our children hurt themselves, we cover their pain with our hands and may even kiss the area better. After lots of hugs and kisses the pain disappears like a miracle and the child is fine.

We all have the ability to heal others and ourselves with our hands and change our lives with the use of this book. I will endeavour to show you how you can transform your life into a more peaceful and productive experience.

We have three levels of existence: Conscious, subconscious and super conscious or divine mind.

The conscious level of awareness is how we associate ourselves to the environment. We experience the environment as an expression of ourselves. All that we are here to learn is within the experience of life – positive and negative. We create all that we experience, with the use of our mind and our perceptions.

The subconscious is our motor; it only wants an easy life and learns survival patterns quickly. These are placed into our day to day level of existence. Always remember, what you say and do is retained in the subconscious mind,

The divine level of awareness is our Eternal Spirit; this is our higher consciousness and knows all. This is our true self of total love and acceptance.

The grounding technique

This is used to heal yourself through your inner mind and prepare you for a healing. It is a tool that is used to clear the issues you carry around day to day.

NOTE: Please read this section through first, before doing anything – understanding that this will be collected and absorbed by your subconscious mind.

You may find that you will feel different even as you endeavour to go through this visualisation. After reading the instructions do each part in sections, either with your eyes closed or open and focusing on a space about two metres away from you.

Step One

Sit comfortably on the floor or on a chair. (This should only take about five minutes once you are used to the grounding technique).

Step Two

Read the instructions through then close your eyes for one minute.

Step Three

Think of all of the things that are happening to you in your life and around you at the current moment. Then create a colour in your mind and sit with it for approximately one-minute.

Step Four

Imagine that you are breathing in this colour – in through your nose and out through you mouth.

Very soon the subconscious will start to take over and you may find other issues come into your awareness. Take the breath into your upper chest and breathe out any issues from your upper chest. Then take the breath deeper down to your stomach and keep breathing out through your mouth. This will create a more relaxed state of mind.

Step Five

Imagine taking the breath all the way down to your feet and clearing all issues out of your body, with the strength of your breath.

Close your eyes for one minute.

Step Six

Imagine invisible cords or roots flowing out through your feet into the earth. Through these roots we are going to release any negativity or fear, anger, anxiety and anticipation down to the earth.

Step Seven

Imagine all this negative energy flowing out through your body into the centre of the earth.

Close your eyes for one minute.

Step Eight

All energy is transferred, so as you release negative energy to the earth, you will receive positive energy back. Imagine the earth's positive energy flowing up through your feet, your legs, your torso, and your arms, all the way to the top of the head.

Close eyes for one minute.

Step Nine

Imagine a white light above the top of your head. Imagine this light flowing all around you. Bring the light down through the top of your head and flowing all the way down to your feet. This will connect you to your healing energy. As the light flows down to the base of your spine imagine light flowing out down to the earth.

Close your eyes for one minute.

Then slowly bring your awareness back into the room.

Chakra Opening

Chakra opening is a form of healing and protection. The reason we open our chakras is to raise our vibration into a more effective state of awareness and consciousness. We can do this with the strength of our mind. We all have untapped potential that is waiting to be developed to lead us into a more effective, productive lifestyle. We only use a small amount of our brain and with these skills you are developing other sections of your awareness.

Step One

Imagine breathing all the way down to the base of your spine.

There, imagine a red rose opening up from bud to full bloom.

This will be enough to open your base red chakra.

Close your eyes for one minute.

Step Two

Now imagine breathing into your orange chakra.

Place both hands three to four fingers below your belly button and think of the colour orange. This will be enough to open your orange chakra.

Close your eyes for one minute.

Step Three

Now imagine breathing into your yellow chakra.

Place both your hands three to four fingers above your belly button and think of the colour yellow. You can think of a daffodil or anything that you associate with yellow.

Close your eyes for one minute.

Step Four

Now imagine breathing into your green chakra.

Place both hands over your heart and think of the colour green. You can think of a green field or anything that you associate with green.

Close your eyes for one minute.

Step Five

Now imagine breathing into your blue chakra.

Place both your hands over your throat and think of the colour blue.

You can think of a blue sky or anything that you associate with blue.

Close your eyes for one minute.

Step Six

Now imagine breathing into your indigo third eye chakra.

Place both hands over your eyes and think of the colour indigo. You can think of the rich royal colour you can see on a rainbow or anything that you associate with indigo.

Close your eyes for one minute.

Step Seven

Now imagine breathing into your violet crown chakra.

Place both hands over your head in the shape of a pyramid and think of the colour violet.

You can think of a violet flower flowing from bud to full bloom or anything that you can associate with violet.

Close your eyes for one minute.

Hands On Healing with Reiki

To perform a healing session on a client follows the very same principles of the self-attuning process and the grounding technique.

To perform a healing session, place the person on a massage table or lying comfortably on the floor, with a comfortable pillow under their head. The more comfortable the client is the better the treatment. In fact the more comfortable that we are, the better the treatment will be. Always remember to be in a comfortable position, so you are not placing strain on you physical body or feeling uncomfortable during a healing session.

We will all endeavour to give a hundred percent during a healing session as we practice our newfound skills. Always remember that we heal our children without even thinking about it.

Once you have grounded yourself you are now ready to perform a healing session.

The Healing Session

First of all we must state our intention to heal by using an affirmation. This will allow the Reiki energy to start flowing through your body. We are stating to our higher self that it is time to align our self with the Universe and the life force energy that is ours by Divine Right.

Step One

Say: "I desire to be a clear vessel of divine light and wish to heal with Reiki". Imagine white light flowing down through your crown, all the way to your feet.

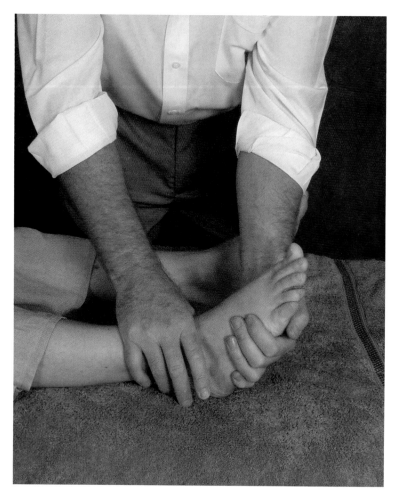

Step Two

First place one hand over the base of the foot and the other over the ankle.

Note: Our left side is our spiritual side if you are right handed and vice-versa if you are left handed. The right side of our body is the physical or control side if you are right handed. We have secondary chakra points that flow all over the body and we have chakras on our hands and on the base of our feet. Our hands and feet also have reflexology points that are connected to every vital organ in the body and we store positive and negative energy in our vital organs.

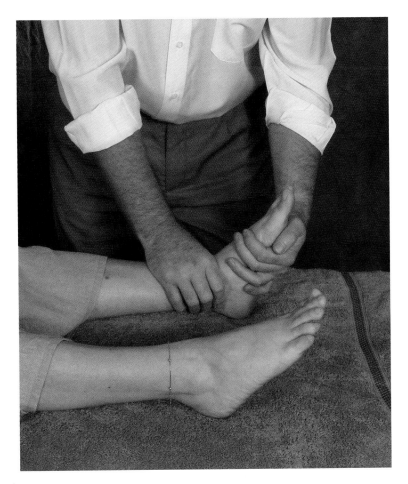

Step Three

Imagine cords of light flowing out from the person's feet, down to the Earth, similar to the grounding meditation that you have done yourself. This will give any trapped energy the ability to be easily directed out of the body, and flow to the Earth, where it can be absorbed and purified. Deep-rooted resentment is held in our ankles and this will allow any trapped energy to flow out through the foot chakra to Earth.

Imagine that you connect the hand covering the ankle to the hand covering the base of the foot, and allow the energy to flow out to the earth.

Close your eyes for one minute.

Repeat with other foot.

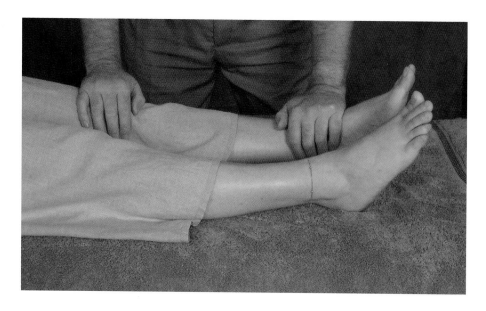

Step Four

Place one hand over the ankle and the other hand over the knee. We hold deep-rooted anger in our knees. Imagine the white light, flowing out through the palms of your hands and going directly through to the knee. Imagine the energy flowing through the calf, to connect to the ankle.

Close your eyes for one minute.

Repeat with other leg.

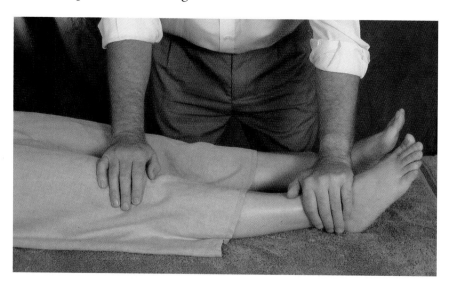

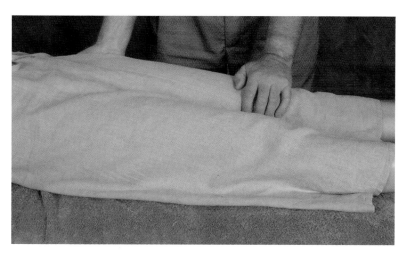

Step Five

Place one hand on the knee and the other on the hip joint or ball joint. We hold any imbalance in our hips. Our legs are our pillars of strength; we keep our past records hidden within the realms of our legs. This is our karmic past, which is positive and negative karma that we have built up throughout our existence.

Imagine the light flowing out through the palm of your hand into the hip, and down through the leg and out through the foot to earth.

Close your eyes for one minute.

Do the same with the other hip and knee.

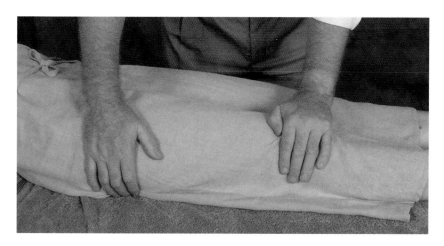

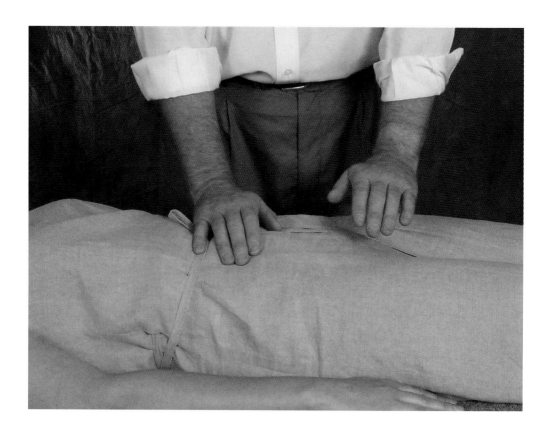

Step Six

Place one hand over the base red chakra and the other over the yellow chakra. Imagine the light flowing out through the palms of your hands and filling the chakras full of light. You can imagine the light filling up a cup that is half empty.

This is connecting the element of Earth to the Divine Spirit that is within us all.

Close your eyes and think of the red and yellow cups full of light. Stop when you have filled both cups with light.

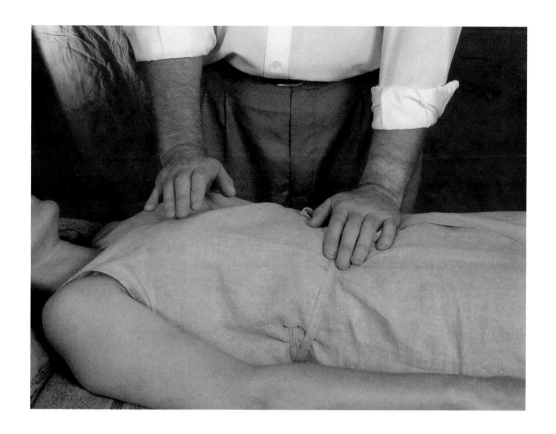

Step Seven

Place one hand over the yellow chakra and the other hand over the green chakra. Imagine light flowing out through the palms of your hands and filling the green chakra full of light.

Imagine light filling up a cup that is half empty. This is connecting the element of the Eternal spirit to the Divine that is within us all.

Close your eyes and think of the cup filling up with light.

Stop when you have filled the green chakra cup with light.

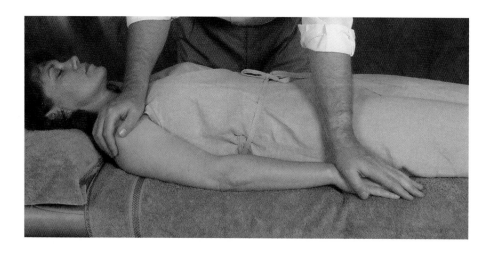

Step Eight

Place one hand over the shoulder and the other hand over the palm of the hand. We hold negative energy in our arms by holding on to tightly to the past. Imagine an invisible cord flowing out through the palm of the hand to Earth. This will allow any trapped energy that is locked within the arm to be released. Close your eyes for one minute and create the cord connecting the palm of the hand to earth with the strength of your mind.

Now imagine the light flowing to the shoulder and out through the hand to earth. Close your eyes and think of the light, clearing out the negative energy, imagine the arm as a clear vessel of light.

Now do the same with the other shoulder and hand.

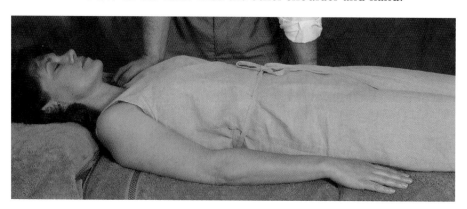

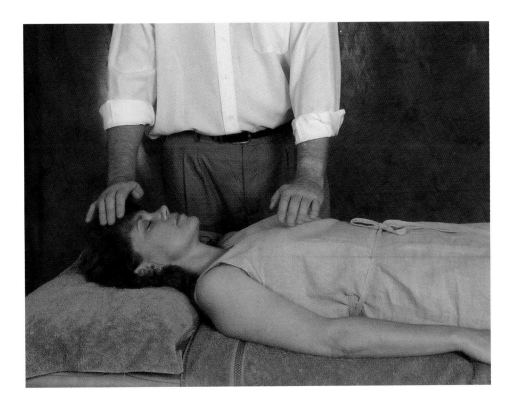

Step Nine

Place one hand over the heart chakra and the other hand over the third eye/crown chakras. Imagine light flowing through your hands and filling the crown chakra with light. This will connect the crown chakra to the light and open the heart chakra. Close your eyes and think of the light, clear any negativity out of the crown chakra.

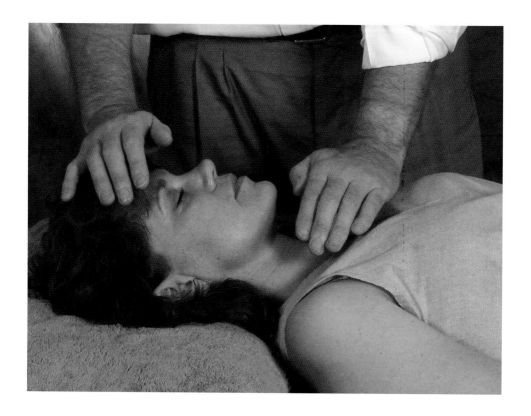

Step Ten

Place one hand over the throat chakra and the other over the third eye/crown chakras. Imagine light flowing out through your hands and filling the throat chakra with light. This will open the throat chakra and release any negativity in relation to communication problems – giving the client the ability to talk from the heart. Close your eyes and imagine the light clearing the negativity out of the throat chakra.

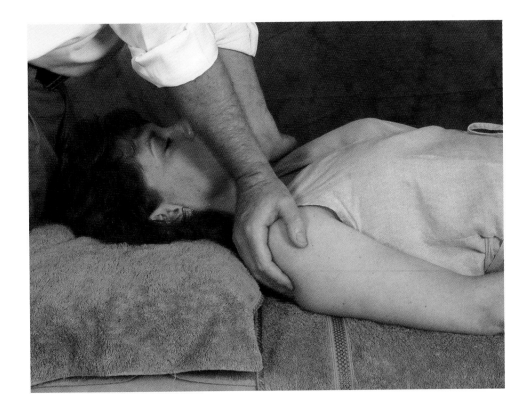

Step Eleven

Place both hands over the shoulders. Imagine the light flowing out through your hands and light flowing all the way through the body to the feet. This will release any negativity that is flowing through the body. Close your eyes and imagine the light flowing through the body until it reaches the feet.

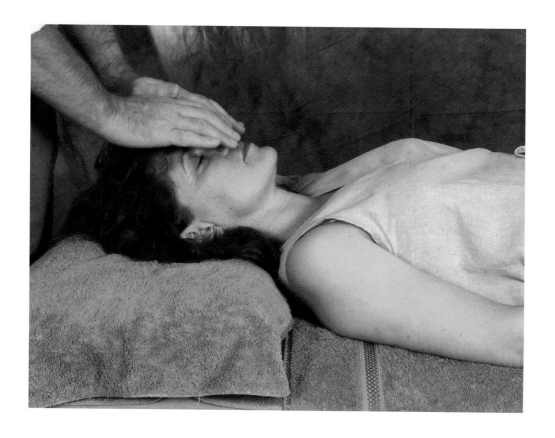

Step Twelve

Place both hands over the eyes. Imagine light flowing though the eyes and third eye, or indigo chakra. This will release any negativity that is connected to thoughts and feelings.

Close your eyes and imagine light filling the third eye chakra until it is full of light.

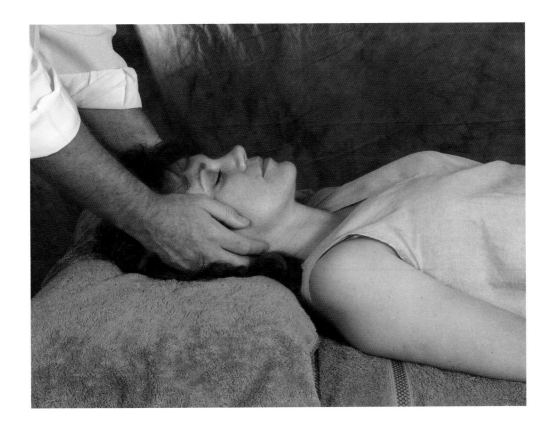

Step Thirteen

Place both hands over the ears. Imagine the light flowing through your hand into the ears. This will clear any negativity that has been heard through life. Close your eyes and imagine the light clearing any negativity from the ears.

Step Fourteen

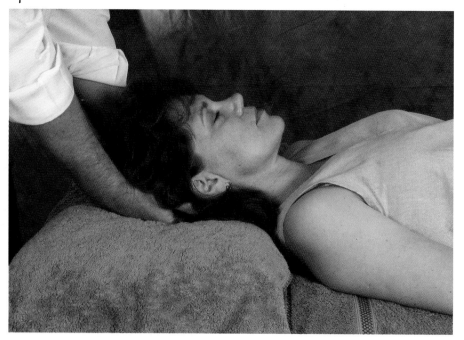

Place both hands behind the head. Place both hands either side of the head and gently rest the head onto one hand and turn the head gently as you move the other hand underneath, so you are supporting the head at all times. Once your hands are gently placed under the head, place your fingers onto the base of the neck and skull.

Imagine the light flowing out through your hands and clearing any residual negativity from the crown and third eye chakra.

Make sure that you have placed your hands under the base of the skull by moving the head gently from one side to the other.

Spinal Problems

The human spinal column runs directly parallel to the Primary Chakra system. We feel pain in our spinal column when our chakra system is low in energy. Filling the chakra cups will give the spinal column the ability to heal itself.

Protection

Protection is used to keep the healing energy flowing through the body. The environment and issues that we face day to day affect us all. This creates stress and pain throughout the body. Once you have finished with your healing, the person you have healed may be going into exactly the same environment that caused the problem in the first place.

Step One

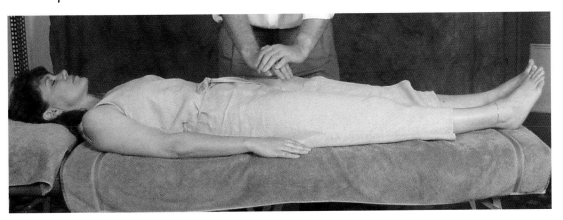

State your intention to protect your client: " I wish to protect …….. with Reiki healing."

Find the centre of the body. Place both hands over the top of each other, and place or draw with the hands a figure eight over the whole body. The figure eight is the Universal sign of infinity and used for protection.

Do this three times.

Step Two

Place both hands over the top of each other and follow the aura level around the body. Say "protect" three times, or "Reiki, Reiki, Reiki."

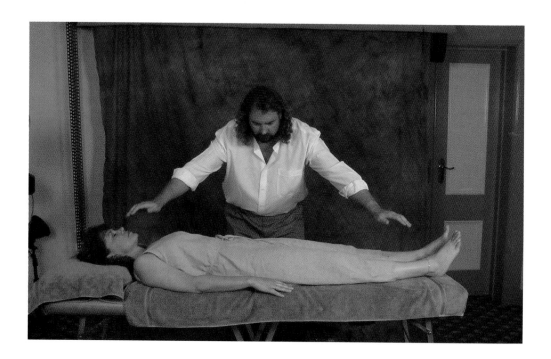

Step Three

Once you are finished protecting your client, thank your Reiki guides for helping you during the healing.

Chapter 7

Greek and Celtic Mythology in Relation to the Body

The Underworld

The underworld, middle world and upper world are all sections of the human body as a cosmic microcosm. In other words the cosmos is flowing through us as we flow through the cosmos.

Imagine a tree with its roots flowing down our legs. The legs retain the sustenance that helps the tree grow strong. Fertile ground will mean that the tree is strong and has good roots into the earth. If the ground is infertile the tree will have poor roots and wind can easily topple the tree. If we experience an infertile environment we have shallow roots and are easily toppled by our thoughts and emotions.

The underworld is the section of the body that lies below our yellow chakra or divine self. This area covers our legs, lower abdominal regions of the body and the red and orange chakras.

The feet are our connection to earth. Imagine the legs as two roman pillars that hold the experience of life. The ankles and knees are release valves that hold the pillars of the under world and carry the energy to move forward throughout life. We have lymphatic points that allow energy to be released from the knees and ankles on a continual basis. The legs are our records of experiences or akashic records. Whatever we experience throughout life is held within the energy of the legs and lower abdomen. Lymphatic drainage is a good remedy to release negative energy held or retained in the legs. The energy is held in the form of lumps underneath the skin and a good massage can relieve negative issues.

If we sustain problems with our feet this is directly associated to stress and worry and directly related to our position on the earth. Dry skin or skin irritations can occur on an infrequent or continual basis. To sustain broken or bruised bones is directly related to how you wish to move from the situation that is currently surrounding you.

We hold deep-rooted resentment in our ankles from the issues sustained from the life that we are currently going though. Deep-rooted resentment can be released by placing light directly into the ankle. The ankle valve is our second segment of operation to the process of records and our deepest records of lives are recorded from just above the ankle to the knee. We hold deep-rooted anger in our knees from the issues sustained from the life we are currently going through.

The knees are our central point of the pillars and hold records that are related to experiences that occurred in the middle of the life process. Deep-rooted anger can be released by placing light into the knee and allowing the anger to flow to earth. The light is positive energy based and will replace the negativity with positive energy flow.

The hips are our balanced section of the body. If we have problems with our feet, ankles or knees this will misalign the hips, and throw out the whole of the spinal column. We hold our balance from the hips.

The Middle World

The middle world is the section of the body that is directly proportional to the yellow chakra, green chakra, blue chakra, and the vital organs. Imagine a tree with the trunk facing the environment and the challenges of time. As the tree grows through each year or cycle it has a ring of existence that shows the experiences and weather patterns within the tree itself. Similar to the way experiences that we go through in life show in our body in the form of pain and ill health.

The effects of the middle world journey shows in our heart, lungs, throat, spleen, spinal column, shoulders, arms, intestines, and gall bladder. Anything to do with negative issues experienced throughout this life will show in the vital organs. The spinal column is also affected by any negative issues that are experienced throughout the middle world. Draining energy from the primary chakra system will cause pain in the spinal column.

The Upper World

The upper world is the base of the skull, the third eye chakra, and crown chakra. Imagine a tree with the branches flowing out from the trunk of the tree with leaves extending out to the sunlight. The tree transfers the light into energy through the leaves that flows throughout the whole of the tree. We are connected to light through our crown chakra and this light flows though the whole of the body. The light flows with the use of our thoughts and feelings. The light flows down our kundalini to our roots or earth.

If we have a blocked primary chakra system this will inhibit the flow of energy causing pain in the body. The energy flows out from our primary chakra system to the meridian system and feeds the energy to the whole of the body. Our thoughts are similar to the leaves on a tree. Some thoughts we hold on to and see as goals or ambition or beliefs. As the leaves shed from the tree we have to continually change or strengthen our beliefs of ourselves directly related to the environment. What we value and believe about ourselves positively or negatively will expose us to the environment.

We have the freedom of choice and free will to experience this life as we choose. Life is a gift from God; the light of God is there for all of us to rise up into with the branches of our mind. We are as necessary to God as God is to us – for human beings are the channels to bring the plan to pass.

Go into life with love for yourself and others. The environment is a reflection of us. Whatever we say or do is reflected back at us in the form of experience. If you show love and compassion to yourself and others, this will be reflected back in a positive way to you. Accept nothing but love and acceptance for yourself. Reject anger, fear, and living negatively. We are not trees; we don't have roots that secure us in the same position throughout our existence. If we are not happy with our environment, we can move on – change the environment and the way we think. Seek positive people and be positive, accept that all of the things that have happened through our lives happened exactly as they were meant to, and move forward thinking positive thoughts towards yourself and others. Love is the strongest energy of all and we all desire to be loved.

References

Diane Stein *Essential Reiki, A complete guide to an ancient healing art.* The Crossing Press Inc., Freedom, CA 1995.

Acknowledgments

This book could not have been written without the help of so many people. I want to express my gratitude to the following:

To everyone I have met as I have trodden my life's path. Each one of you has provided me something to help me reach a greater understanding of myself.

To the people of Adelaide, Australia, a place I regard as my University of Life: Thank you for the opportunity to learn many special lessons.

To Karen, my friend and partner: Thank you for your support during the writing of this book and the patience to see the potential in me.

To the people of New South Wales who have shown me such kindness as I have travelled my journey. Also to Janita – who I consider as my Australian mother – and her family: Thank you for believing in me, helping me realise my potential and letting me stay in your home to write this book.

To my children, Allan and Anthony: Thank you for our patience as I have travelled the world in search of the truth. I love you both.

To Sharni, the Crystal Wizard : Special thanks for helping me to get this book off the ground and helping me in so many ways.

Encyclopedia of Thai Massage

A Complete Guide to Traditional Thai Massage Therapy
and Acupressure

by C. Pierce Salguero

Thai massage is an increasingly popular healing modality and this book, as its title suggests, is the single most informative and comprehensive book on Thai massage ever written. At least an introductory course in Thai Massage has become a prerequisite in many American and European massage schools, and a growing number of massage therapists and yoga practitioners are looking for high-quality information on this ancient art.

This book is based on the author's experience teaching in Thailand's most prestigious massage school (the Shivagakomarpaj Institute), and at his school in the U.S. (The Tao Mountain School of Thai Massage and Herbal Medicine), as well as from his seven years of practice as a Thai therapist. The work also draws heavily from the author's life in Thailand as a researcher of traditional medicine, as well as his six years of experience with the practice of Hatha Yoga.

Drawing from Thai history, cultural studies, Buddhist religion, and yogic practices, as well a modern understanding of anatomy and physiology, this book finally bridges the gap between the theory and practice of Thai massage. The Encyclopedia of Thai Massage is unique in that it presents this form of bodywork as it is understood in Thailand, as a therapeutic medical science.

With more than 200 photographs and diagrams, which beautifully and clearly illustrate the points made in the text, everyone will enjoy and benefit from this unique volume, whatever their level of experience.

C. Pierce Salguero studied Thai massage and traditional herbalism from 1997 to 2001 under Lek Chaiya, Baan Nit, the Shivagakomarpaj Traditional Medicine Hospital, and other renowned teachers in Chiang Mai, Thailand. He returned to the US in 2001 to found the Tao Mountain School of Traditional Thai Massage and Herbal Medicine in Charlottesville, Virginia. For more information visit taomountain.org

Published by FINDHORN PRESS • ISBN 1-84409-029-9
available from your local bookstore
or directly from www.findhornpress.com

Anything Can Be Healed
by Martin Brofman

"I released myself from a terminal illness which traditional medicine
had considered hopeless – untreatable – and returned to perfect health.
I believe we are all healers,
and somewhere deep inside we know that anything can be healed."

Martin Brofman has developed a system of healing that effectively and seamlessly blends Western psychology and Eastern philosophies. His groundbreaking work on chakras and their connection to both mind and body allows us to read the body as a map of the consciousness, tracking routes from symptoms through to causes and then working with them. Learn these techniques and you may well nip in the bud potential future ailments, too.

Anything Can be Healed explores the ideas that 'how' we are physically is a reflection of 'who' we are and 'how' our life is. It empowers us to make changes and to take responsibility for our health and well-being. Martin is living proof of the power of his own techniques.

Published by FINDHORN PRESS • ISBN 1-84409-016-7
available from your local bookstore
or directly from www.findhornpress.com

About Findhorn Press...

Findhorn Press was born in 1971 when the demand for the guidance of Eileen Caddy (one of the founders of the world famous Findhorn community) was so great that it was decided to publish it as a bound book: *God Spoke to Me* was launched and is still in print today! This was followed by many other books by Eileen Caddy, as well as several meditations tapes. Her latest title is the new (2002) expanded version of her autobiography, *Flight Into Freedom and Beyond*.

In 1994 Findhorn Press was purchased by Thierry and Karin Bogliolo, two long-term community members, and it has been run and developed as an independent publishing house since then. Its main office is still on the Findhorn campus but thanks to high speed internet connections several of its employees live in other parts of the world.

Findhorn Press has grown tremendously since it became independent, and publishes works by Diana Cooper, Martin Brofman, James F. Twyman, Marko Pogacnik, Darren Main, John Stowe, Jack Temple, David Lawson, Judy Hall and many others. While many of our authors are living or have lived in the Findhorn community, the others share the spiritual vision which is congruent with its core principles and practices.

Findhorn Press strives to bring healing and hope into our world. We seek to inspire and educate and inform our readers in every corner of the Earth – many of our books are published in several languages. Thank you for joining us on our journey into a positive and heart-centered future.

www.findhornpress.com

For further information about the Findhorn Foundation and the Findhorn Community, please contact:

Findhorn Foundation

The Visitors Centre
The Park, Findhorn IV36 3TZ, Scotland, UK
tel 01309 690311
enquiries@findhorn.org
www.findhorn.org

For a complete Findhorn Press catalogue, please contact:

Findhorn Press

305a The Park, Findhorn
Forres IV36 3TE
Scotland, UK
tel 01309 690582
fax 01309 690036
info@findhornpress.com
www.findhornpress.com